W9-CCC-733

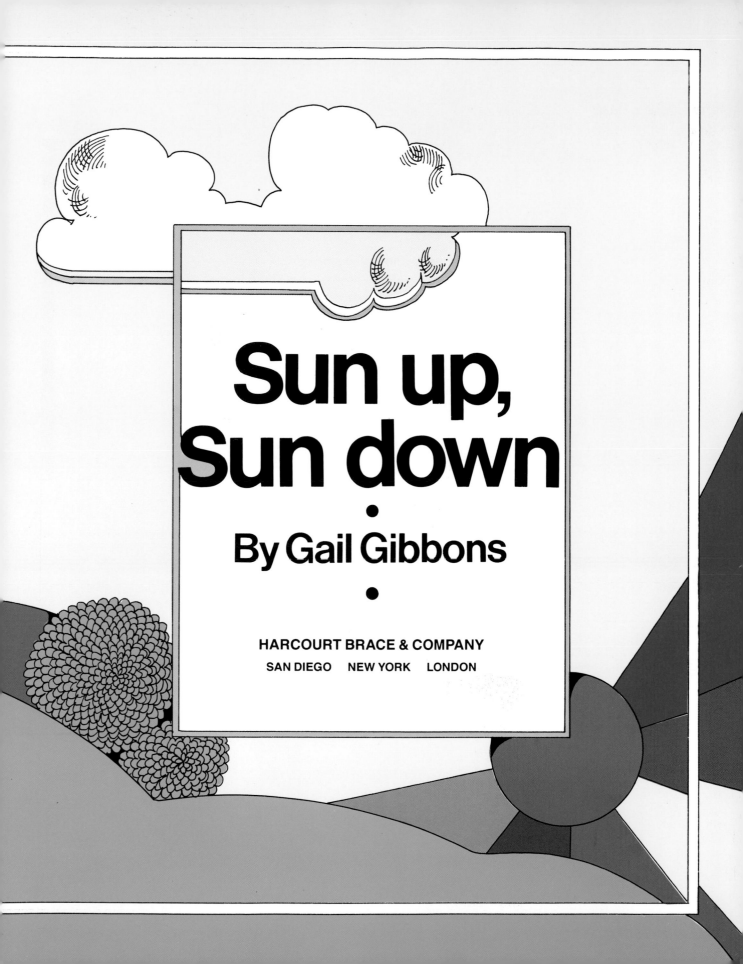

Sun up,
Sun down

•

By Gail Gibbons

•

HARCOURT BRACE & COMPANY

SAN DIEGO   NEW YORK   LONDON

FOR FLORENCE ALEXANDER

For his help, special thanks to Michael Heeremans
of the Chelsea School, Vermont

Copyright © 1983 by Gail Gibbons

All rights reserved. No part of this publication may be reproduced or
transmitted in any form or by any means, electronic or mechanical,
including photocopy, recording, or any information storage and retrieval
system, without permission in writing from the publisher.

Requests for permission to make copies of any part of the work
should be mailed to the following address:
Permissions Department, Harcourt, Inc.,
6277 Sea Harbor Drive, Orlando, Florida 32887-6777.

Library of Congress Cataloging-in-Publication Data
Gibbons, Gail. Sun up, sun down.
SUMMARY: Describes the characteristics of the sun
and the ways in which it regulates life on earth.
1. Sun—Pictorial works—Juvenile literature. [1. Sun.] I. Title.
QB521.5.G5 1983 523.7 82-23420
ISBN 0-15-282781-1
ISBN 0-15-282782-X (pb)
Printed by South China Printing Co., Ltd., Hong Kong

G I K M O P N L J H
Printed in Hong Kong

The sun wakes me up. It rises in the east and shines
through my window.

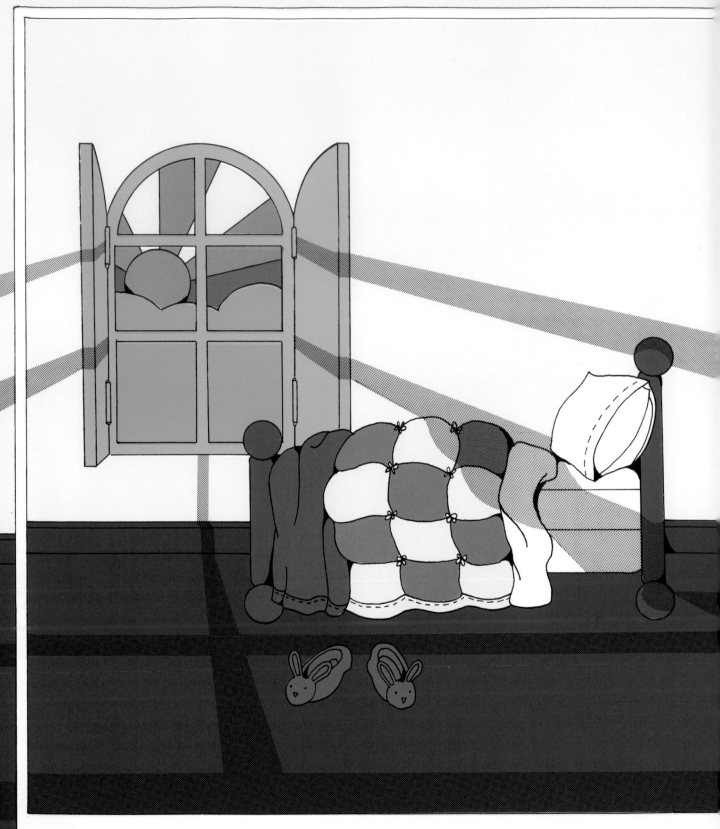

It lights up my room . . .

and makes patterns on my floor.

Its brightness colors the clouds and the sky, but the sun itself . . .

is too bright to look at. It could hurt my eyes.

I go down to breakfast. My cereal is made of wheat. My dad tells me the sun made the wheat grow.

He says the sun gives power and energy to make plants and trees grow big and tall.

It is summer. Because it is hot, I don't need to wear a coat or sweater today. The sun is high in the sky, and the days are long.

When the sun is low in the sky, the days are shorter. It is winter, and it is cold. That is when I need my coat, hat, and mittens.

But on a summer morning like this, I see my shadow on the ground. The sun is behind me in the east. When I move, my shadow moves, too. It points west.

By noontime, the sun is shining right above me. My shadow is gone. It is a hot time of day, and I am glad when my mother calls me inside for lunch.

While I'm eating, I ask my parents a question. "How far away is the sun?"
My mother tells me it is very far away . . . 93 million miles from our planet, earth.

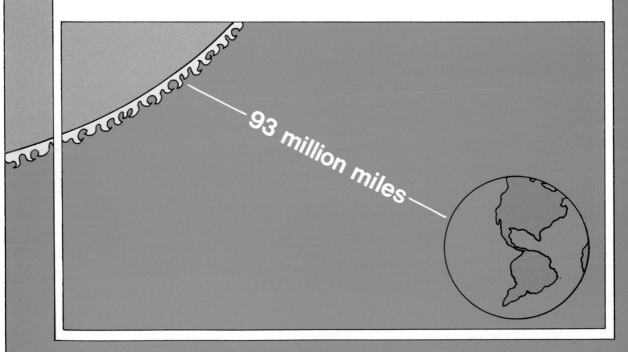

93 million miles

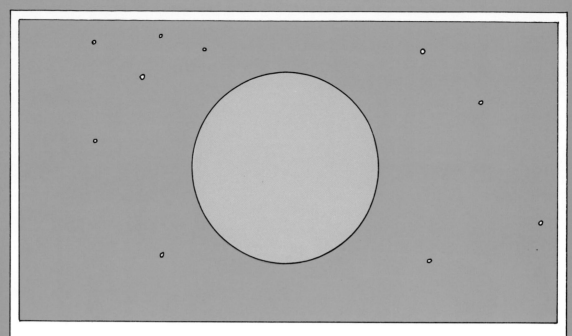

She says it is a very big star. It looks bigger than the other stars because it is closer to us.
My dad says the sun is a ball of very hot, glowing gases.
It keeps our planet warm.

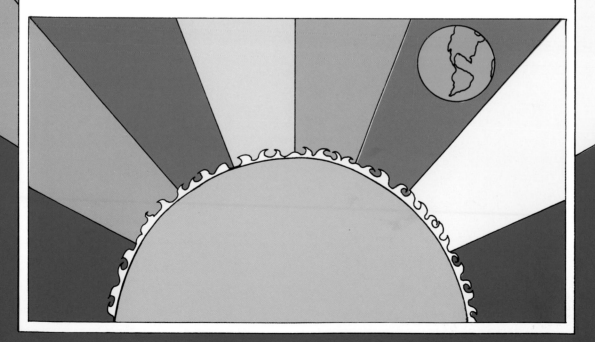

He says our earth would be dark and very cold if there were no sun. It would also be empty. Nothing could live on it.

After lunch I go outside. My shadow is back again, but now it points east. The sun is moving west behind me.

Suddenly big clouds begin to cover the sun. My shadow is gone again. Over in the valley, the sun peeks through the clouds, making shadows on the ground.

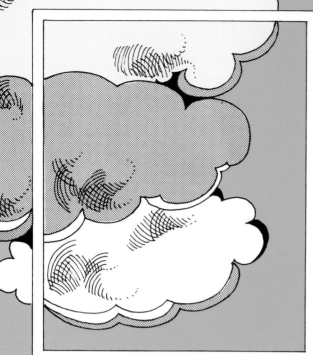

More clouds come. They are gray and black. It becomes dark. A raindrop hits my nose, and I run home.

I hear the rain on the roof of my house. My dad says the sun helps make rain so that we can have fresh water to drink and so that plants and trees can grow.

He tells me that when the sun shines on our oceans, lakes, and rivers, it warms the water. Some of the water turns into vapor and rises high into the sky.

The cooler air up in the sky turns the vapor into tiny rain-drops. Clouds are formed. The raindrops float higher up into colder air. They become bigger and bigger. Finally, when the drops are heavy and big enough, the drops fall and it rains.

Soon the storm clouds begin to drift away. Although it is still sprinkling, the sun appears once again and shines through the raindrops. I see a beautiful rainbow. My mom says the light of the sun shining through the raindrops makes the rainbow.

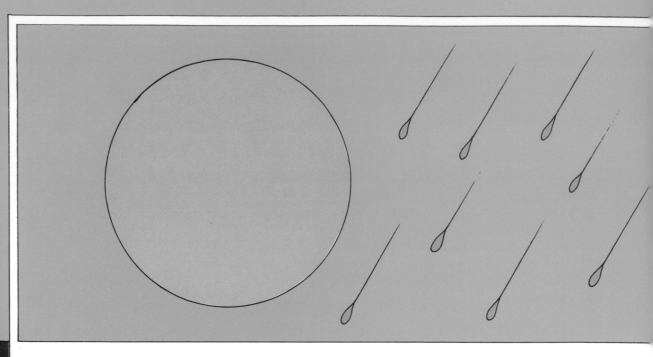

She tells me the sunlight looks white, but it really isn't. It is made up of many colors. When a beam of light shines through a glass triangle, called a prism, the beam of light is bent.

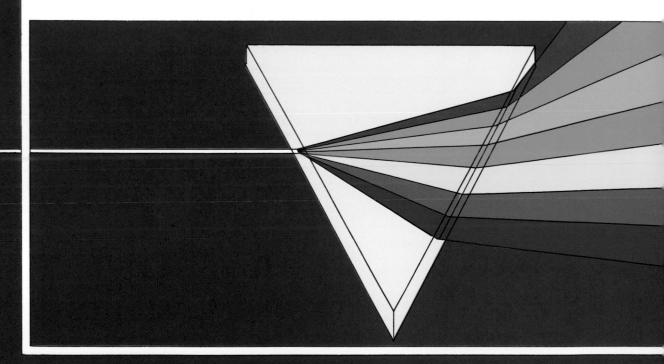

Some of the rays of the beam bend more than others, separating the light into different colors. The drops of water are like the prism. When sunbeams shine through the raindrops, what we see is a rainbow.

When I go outside, my shadow is long and skinny. The sun is setting in the western sky.

It is getting cool outside. The sun is leaving for today, and the sky is getting dark.

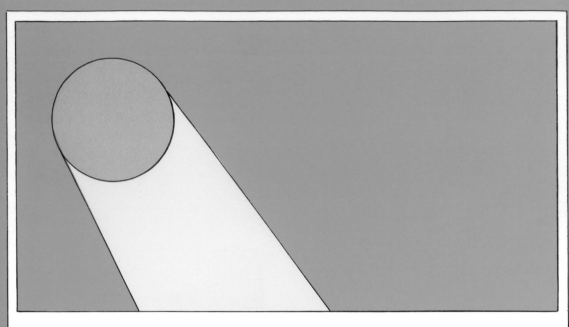

My dad tells me the sun will shine on the other side of our planet while I'm asleep. He says the earth spins round and round and makes a complete turn once every twenty-four hours. When our part of the earth faces the sun, it is day. When it is turned away from the sun, it is night.

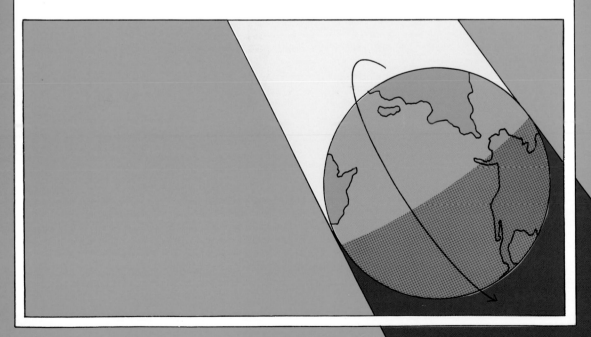

It is night now. The sun is down. The sky is dark.
It is time to sleep.

Some Sunny Facts

 The sun is 400 times farther away from the earth than the moon.

 If our sun were hollow, it could hold one million of our earths.

 Every once in a while, the moon passes between the sun and the earth. Such an event is called a solar eclipse.

 Our sun is nearly five billion years old.

 Some people use the sun's energy to heat their water and their homes.

 The world's largest solar power plant is in the Mojave Desert in California.

J523.7   Gibbons, Gail.
GIB
C·l   Sun up, sun down.

$16.00

DATE			
APR 1 1 2003			

BAKER & TAYLOR